A Whale of a Tale

By Captain Robert R. Singleton Ph.D.

Illustrated by Kylie Scheir

A WHALE OF A TALE

Copyright © 2023 Captain Robert R. Singleton, Ph.D.

Illustrations by Kylie Scheir

1210 SW 23rd PL • Ocala, FL 34471 • Phone 352-622-1825
Website: www.atlantic-pub.com • Email: sales@atlantic-pub.com
SAN Number: 268-1250

No part of this publication may be reproduced, stored in a retrieval system, or transmitted in any form or by any means, electronic, mechanical, photocopying, recording, scanning, or otherwise, except as permitted under Section 107 or 108 of the 1976 United States Copyright Act, without the prior written permission of the Publisher. Requests to the Publisher for permission should be sent to Atlantic Publishing Group, Inc., 1210 SW 23rd PL, Ocala, Florida 34471.

Library of Congress Control Number: 2023910256

This is a work of fiction. Names, characters, businesses, places, events, locales, and incidents are either the products of the author's imagination or used in a fictitious manner. Any resemblance to actual persons, living or dead, or actual events is purely coincidental.

Printed in the United States

PROJECT MANAGER: Crystal Edwards
INTERIOR LAYOUT AND JACKET DESIGN: Nicole Sturk

This book is dedicated to
Elizabeth Gondek

The purpose of this children's book is to create a desire to learn more about the subject.

It is designed to foster a sense of wonder and journey into an enjoyable adventure. Hopefully to fan a spark of interest to flame that leads the child on a quest for more knowledge. A soul thrust for the subject at hand. The primary job of the instructor is to generate that spark.

Your opinions and ideas regarding this work will be deeply appreciated.

Thank you!

About the Author

Captain Robert R. Singleton Ph.D. is an oceanographer and a merchant marine officer with over 40 years' experience. He has authored six books and several articles. He has also lectured at numerous colleges throughout New England. Captain Singleton is private pilot, has served his country as a decorated paratrooper with the 101st airborne division. He is married with children and grandchildren, he and resides with his family in Western Massachusetts.

About the Illustrator

Kylie Veronica Scheir is an artist with over 10 years of experience. She specializes in henna body art. She also has experience with dance and teaching young children the art that is dance. Kylie is the youngest of three children to her loving, supporting parents. Music is also one of her passions as she plays the piano, guitar, ukulele and flute. She is self-taught in both art and music. Kylie was born in and raised throughout New York State and traveled to Massachusetts to achieve her goal of exploring the world and teaching people about the arts.

Now, old King Neptune
From deep in sea
Called out to his mermaids
To issue a decree.

"Now, my children," he said,
"I've taken a notion
To send out my whales
To explore all my oceans."

"Which whales will go?"
Asked his mermaids in reply.
"There are so many
You cannot deny."

"I'll send Wilson, Lumpus,
Bumpus, and Clyde
For they know the way
To all the seas far and wide."

"They will take a count
Of all my sons and daughters
Who live far and wide
In my deep blue-green waters."

The first one they met

Off the sea of Japan

Was Jilly the Jellyfish

And his quivering band.

They counted their numbers

For there were so many.

And the plankton they feed on

Were more than plenty.

Then off to Australia
In the great Coral Sea
They saw hundreds of sharks
That were hungry as can be!

Then on to New Zealand

In the big Pacific Ocean

There were large schools of dolphins and porpoises

To such a degree.

They jumped and played

For all to see.

Now, Silver the Seahorse
And his friends were at play
When the four friendly whales
Came along their way.

"Where are you going?"
The seahorse exclaimed.
"Why, we're going to meet our friends
Off the coast of Spain."

"May we come along?
For we have a notion
We will make new friends
In that far away ocean."

Now on the way to Mandalay

Where the flying fishes often stay

The whales stopped to spend some time

And watch them at their amazing play.

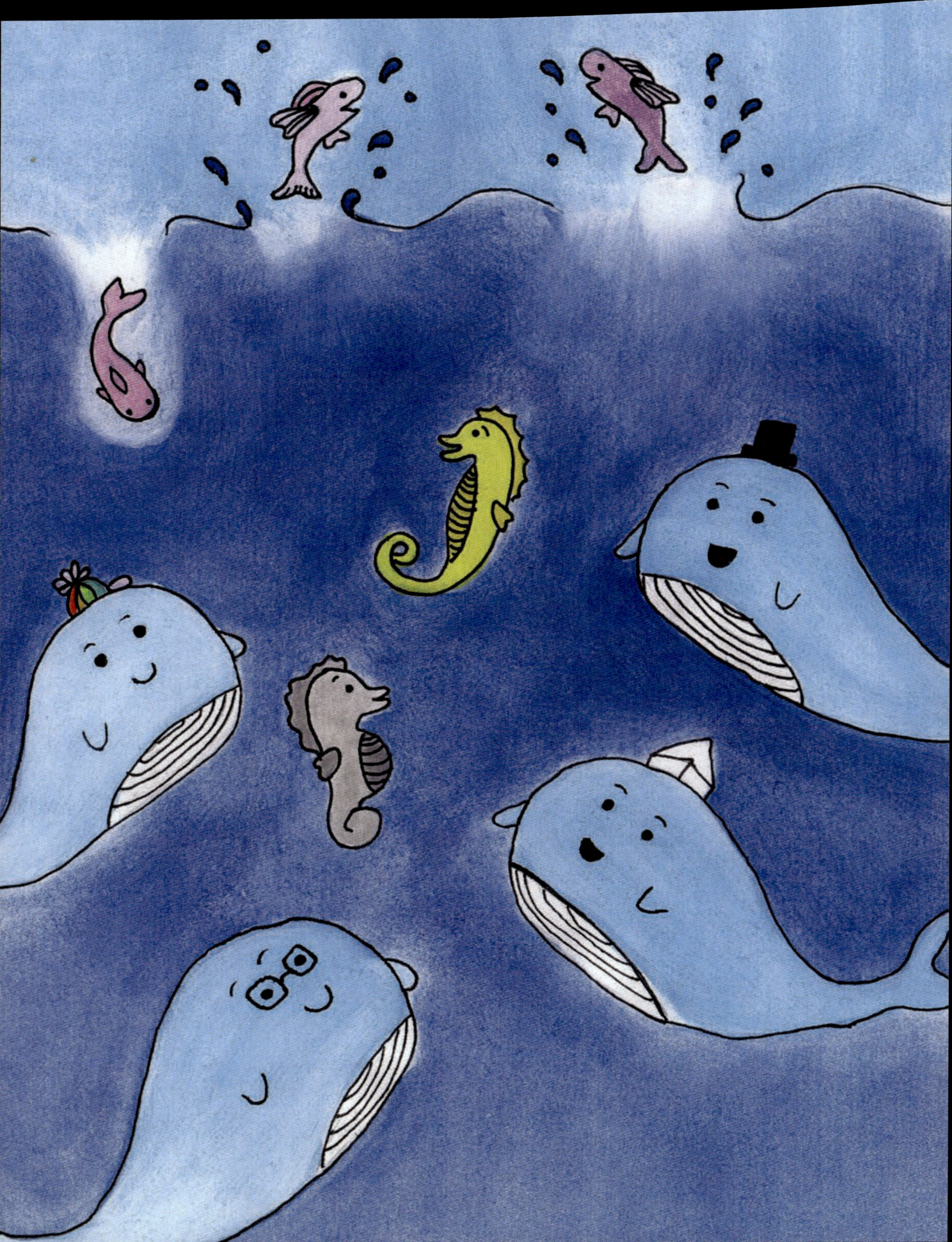

A little while later,
Off the mouth of the Nile,
They met Ruben and his family
Of big crocodiles.

"We will visit you again!"
They said sometime later.
"But now we're off to the Caribbean
To see your cousin, the alligator."

Then, on to New England.

They found it not odd.

They were greeted by Henry the Haddock

And Clarence the Cod.

"We're off to the north
To the Bay of Fundy.
We want to attend the Walrus Festival
Next Monday!"

"Not to worry,"
Said Skylar the Seagull.
"I'll show you the way
In plenty of time for that happy day."

On the way to the Arctic,

Along its icy shores,

They met the penguins, whom they admire

For they were dressed in their formal attire.

It was in the far Arctic,

Where the icebergs float,

The met Sally the Seal

In a place so remote.

"Keep going north," she said,
"And don't stop trying. You
Will see Peter the Polar Bear
And his friend Lenny the Sea Lion."

Now, in the cold, green seas,
The whales did roam.
They met lobsters and crabs
In their deep-water home.

Then, in the evening,
As they passed overhead,
They saw all the clams and oysters
Asleep in their beds.

Now, Skylar the Seagull and Terry the Tern

Were following the whales from above.

They were singing and crying

Out a song that they loved.

Then Nelson the Narwhal,

Was the last to see

The whales when they left

The far northern seas.

"We are going south to meet
With our sons and daughters,
And truly enjoy
the deep warmer waters."

It was through all the oceans

The whales did roam,

Until the mermaids came

And summoned them home.

Then Wilson, Lumpus,
Bumpus, and Clyde
Returned to the place
Where King Neptune resides.

"You have done a fine job,"

The king did decree,

"A great service to all my subjects

In the oceans and seas."

"I'll call you again

If ever I have a notion

To have you again explore

All my seas and oceans."

Made in the USA
Middletown, DE
12 August 2024